For the Bunters

Published by G. Whizzard Publications Ltd.
in association with André Deutsch Ltd., 1978
105 Great Russell Street, London WC1 3LJ.

Colour separation by Colour Craftsmen.
Printed in Italy by New Interlitho (S.p.A.).

ISBN 233 96993 4

△ G. Whizzard/André Deutsch ⊕

Fun Food Feasts

By Nanette Newman
Illustrated by Alan Cracknell.

THE STAFF OF THE FUN FOOD FACTORY INVITE YOU TO ATTEND ONE OR MORE OF THEIR FUN FOOD FEASTS.

Note to Factory Members

Remember, you don't always have to have party feasts
given *for* you. In fact, some of the best parties
are the ones you organize yourself. And the preparation
can be as much fun as the occasion itself.

What is a Party?

A party is when two or more people get together and have fun.

FACTORY RULES

*Make sure you have permission to cook from the factory manager (usually called a mother), or whoever owns the kitchen.

*Always wash your hands first.

*Only use ingredients that are fresh and natural. Nothing artificial – no preservatives, colourings or flavourings; nothing out of a tin. Use *wholemeal* flour, *brown* sugar, *sunflower* oil and *brown* rice whenever possible.

*Get all the right ingredients together *before* you start. And never waste food; it's expensive.

*Remember that hot things can burn you, fat can spit at you, knives can cut you, and boiling water can scald you – Look out for this sign.

*Be careful when using kitchen gadgets – they can be dangerous – and never touch an electric plug with wet hands.

*Wear an apron or overall to protect your clothes.

*Clear up after you.

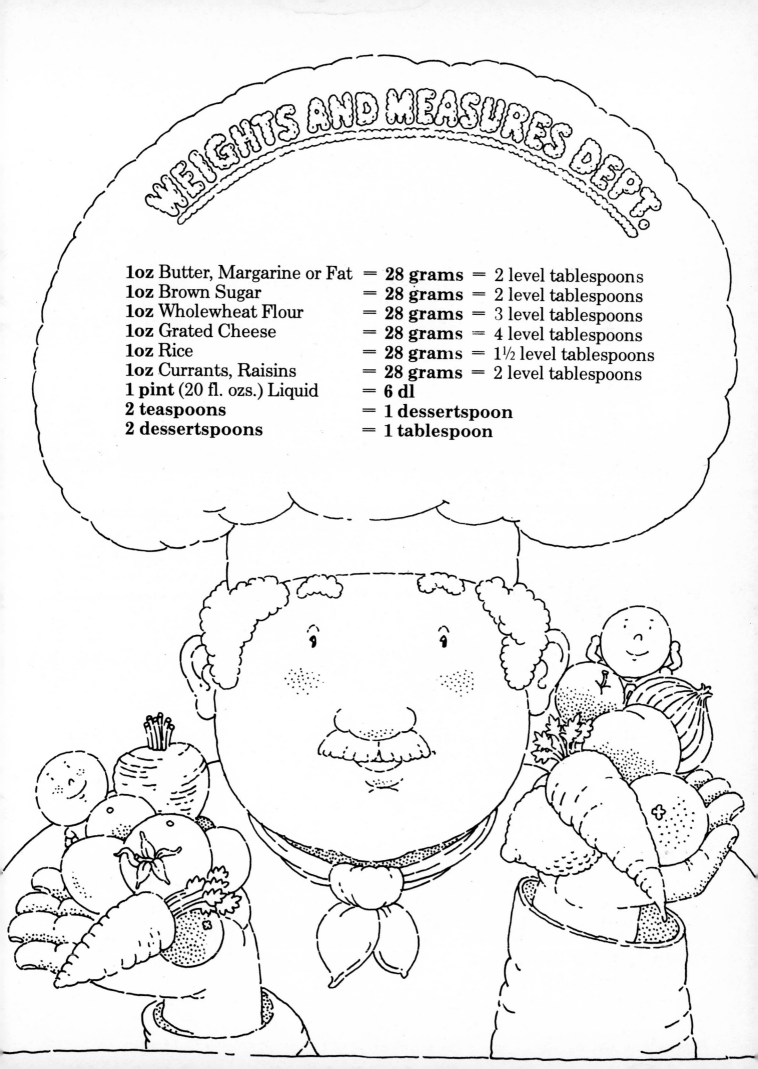

1oz Butter, Margarine or Fat	= **28 grams**	= 2 level tablespoons
1oz Brown Sugar	= **28 grams**	= 2 level tablespoons
1oz Wholewheat Flour	= **28 grams**	= 3 level tablespoons
1oz Grated Cheese	= **28 grams**	= 4 level tablespoons
1oz Rice	= **28 grams**	= 1½ level tablespoons
1oz Currants, Raisins	= **28 grams**	= 2 level tablespoons
1 pint (20 fl. ozs.) Liquid	= **6 dl**	
2 teaspoons	= **1 dessertspoon**	
2 dessertspoons	= **1 tablespoon**	

MAD HATTERS TEA PARTY

All guests come wearing the maddest clothes.
Then you do everything the wrong way round.
Like serving the food under the table instead of on
it. Or playing games where the loser is the winner.
And so on.

Mad Hatters Cabbage Pie

Ingredients

12 large outside cabbage leaves (washed)
A mixture of any of the following, adding up to
4 large cupfuls

Carrots
Peas
Parsnips
Spinach
⚠ Leeks
Onions   } cooked and
Cabbage   chopped up
Beans
Brussels sprouts
Potatoes

3 eggs
4 oz (113 gms) grated cheddar cheese (optional)
⅓ pint (2 dl) milk
Salt and pepper to taste
Dessertspoon of parsley, chives or mint (optional)

Take cabbage leaves and remove really thick
stems. Cook in boiling salted water until just tender
and limp. But *not* soggy. Butter a 10 inch (25 cm)
or thereabouts quiche or tart dish. Line it with
drained cabbage leaves, overlapping and hanging
over the edge.
Put mixed vegetables into a bowl with a dash of salt
and pepper. In another bowl, beat eggs, add grated
cheese and milk, herbs, salt and pepper. And mix
well. Then pour over vegetables. Mix again.
Put into cabbage-lined dish and carefully fold over
cabbage leaves so that the vegetables are
completely enclosed.

Now bake at 375° (Gas mark 5) for about
30 minutes.

⚠ Get someone to help you turn it out
into a serving dish.

Maddeningly delicious hot or cold.

Serves 10.

SHIPWRECK PARTY

Pretend that you and your friends are marooned on a desert island. What would you do about food and shelter – and how would you try to escape? The one with the best ideas gets a prize.

Castaways Bread

Ingredients

1½ lb (.75 kg) flour
1 pint (6 dl) tepid water (just under)
1 dessertspoon sugar (or honey)
1 dessertspoon salt
½ oz (14 gms) yeast
4 oz (113 gms) cheese

Mix yeast and sugar with ¼ pint (1.5 dl) of tepid water in a small jug. Leave somewhere warm till it froths. Pour into flour, then add *almost* all the rest of the water.
Mix well.
Knead. If too dry, add a little more water.
Add most of grated cheese.
Knead again.
Put into greased loaf tin (or make into hamburger bun size).
Cover with a damp tea towel.
Leave to rise for 20 minutes.
Sprinkle top with more grated cheese.

Bake for 40 – 50 minutes at 400° (Gas mark 6).

Make Castaways Sandwiches.

Fish Fish

Ingredients

1 cup any cooked fish (flaked, no skin or bones)
1 cup mashed potato
1 grated carrot
1 egg
Salt/pepper
1 teaspoon of your favourite herb

Mix till well blended. Then make into fish shapes. Melt together in a pan 1 dessertspoon oil and 1 dessertspoon butter.
⚠ Cook fish on both sides until lightly browned. Serve on sea of chopped watercress. Make an 'eye' for the fish with a nut or piece of vegetable.

Serves 2–4 (depending on the size of the fishes).

Have a treasure hunt.

A party for after a match, or when watching a big sporting event on television.

Footballers Filler

Ingredients

4 handfuls brown rice
1 onion
1 tablespoon oil
1 lb (0.5 kg) minced beef
1 lb (0.5 kg) tomatoes
1 oz (28 gms) butter
1 oz (28 gms) flour
½ pint (3 dl) milk
5 oz (140 gms) grated cheese
Salt/pepper
Herbs of your own choice i.e. chives, parsley

 Chop onion and cook gently in tablespoon of oil till soft.
Add the minced beef.
Cook till it is no longer red.
Then add tomatoes (either chopped finely or pulverised in blender).
Add teaspoon of salt, dash of pepper, and teaspoon of chives or parsley or basil.
Leave to simmer gently on low heat.

 Into a large pan of boiling water, add 4 handfuls of rice. Cook till *just* tender, then drain.
Using same saucepan:
Melt the butter, add the flour and mix well.
 Add the milk. Keep stirring over low heat till thick.
Add 4 oz grated cheese. Stir till melted.
Add a dash of salt and pepper.

Spread half the meat mixture into oven-proof dish. Then spread the rice over this. Then the rest of the meat. Pour over the cheese sauce, sprinkle 1 oz grated cheese on top and a sprinkling of herbs.

Bake at 350° (Gas mark 4) for 40 minutes, or until lightly brown and bubbly on top.

Serves 6.

Start your own F.F.F. team.

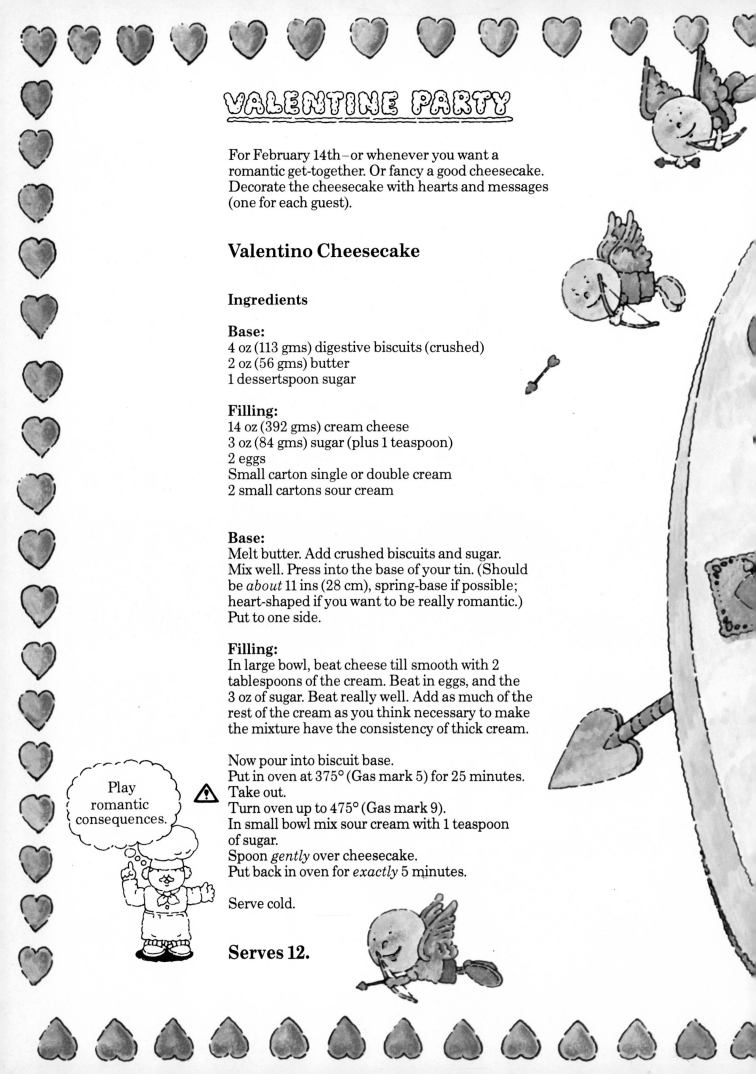

VALENTINE PARTY

For February 14th – or whenever you want a romantic get-together. Or fancy a good cheesecake. Decorate the cheesecake with hearts and messages (one for each guest).

Valentino Cheesecake

Ingredients

Base:
4 oz (113 gms) digestive biscuits (crushed)
2 oz (56 gms) butter
1 dessertspoon sugar

Filling:
14 oz (392 gms) cream cheese
3 oz (84 gms) sugar (plus 1 teaspoon)
2 eggs
Small carton single or double cream
2 small cartons sour cream

Base:
Melt butter. Add crushed biscuits and sugar. Mix well. Press into the base of your tin. (Should be *about* 11 ins (28 cm), spring-base if possible; heart-shaped if you want to be really romantic.) Put to one side.

Filling:
In large bowl, beat cheese till smooth with 2 tablespoons of the cream. Beat in eggs, and the 3 oz of sugar. Beat really well. Add as much of the rest of the cream as you think necessary to make the mixture have the consistency of thick cream.

Now pour into biscuit base.
Put in oven at 375° (Gas mark 5) for 25 minutes. Take out.
Turn oven up to 475° (Gas mark 9).
In small bowl mix sour cream with 1 teaspoon of sugar.
Spoon *gently* over cheesecake.
Put back in oven for *exactly* 5 minutes.

Serve cold.

Play romantic consequences.

Serves 12.

SWOP CIRCLE

Everyone brings things they would like to swop (books, toys etc.). Lay everything out in a circle on the floor – and let the bargaining begin. All help with the cooking, then swop the Swopburgers as well.

Swopburgers

Ingredients

1 lb (.5 kg) minced beef
4 tablespoons finely chopped onion
2 teaspoons any herbs
2 skinned tomatoes, chopped
Salt/pepper
1 grated raw carrot
4 oz (113 gms) brown breadcrumbs
1 egg
1 tablespoon oil

Mix everything (except the oil) with clean hands or wooden spoon. Heat oil in a large frying pan. Divide mixture into hamburger shapes and put into pan. Brown one side, then turn and cook the other (medium heat).

Keep warm. Serve in bun (your own home-made) or with a salad.

Give each one a different topping.

Suggestions: Cottage cheese, chutney, crushed tomatoes, cheese etc.

Then swop with friends.

Serves 4-6.

Make Surprise Swoppers—
2 burgers with the filling sealed inside

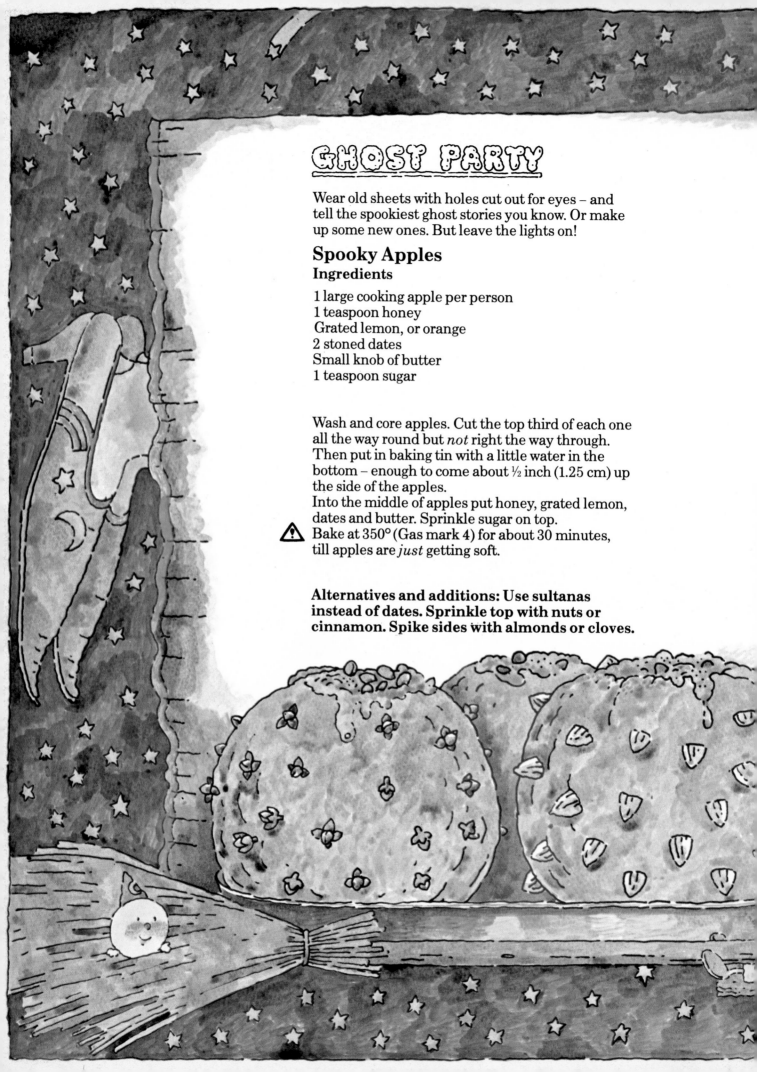

GHOST PARTY

Wear old sheets with holes cut out for eyes – and tell the spookiest ghost stories you know. Or make up some new ones. But leave the lights on!

Spooky Apples
Ingredients

1 large cooking apple per person
1 teaspoon honey
Grated lemon, or orange
2 stoned dates
Small knob of butter
1 teaspoon sugar

Wash and core apples. Cut the top third of each one all the way round but *not* right the way through. Then put in baking tin with a little water in the bottom – enough to come about ½ inch (1.25 cm) up the side of the apples.
Into the middle of apples put honey, grated lemon, dates and butter. Sprinkle sugar on top.
Bake at 350° (Gas mark 4) for about 30 minutes, till apples are *just* getting soft.

Alternatives and additions: Use sultanas instead of dates. Sprinkle top with nuts or cinnamon. Spike sides with almonds or cloves.

Witches Brew

Make a pot of weak tea.
Into each glass put 1 heaped teaspoon of
honey and juice of ½ lemon. When tea is
cool pour it out gradually, stirring till
honey is melted. Put in fridge till cold.

To serve:
Add 2 ice cubes
1 slice of orange
1 sprig of mint
Take a pinch of mixed spices and sprinkle over
the top.

**You can substitute orange juice for lemon
juice, and float sliced apple in it instead of
orange. Also a dash of apple juice is nice.**

TEDDY BEARS PICNIC

Invite lots of young friends to bring their best-loved Teddy Bear for a Teddy Bears Picnic, and 'Best Bear' Competition.

Honey Cake (because bears like honey)

Ingredients

4 oz (113 gms) butter
2 oz (56 gms) sugar
3 tablespoons honey (runny)
2 tablespoons plain yoghurt
2 beaten eggs
8 oz (226 gms) flour, sifted with
3 teaspoons baking powder

Cream butter and sugar together *thoroughly*.
Then mix in honey, beating well.
Add 2 beaten eggs, beat again.
Add 2 tablespoons yoghurt, beat again.
Add sifted flour and baking powder.
Mix. Spoon into greased 7 inch (17.5 cm) cake tin.

Bake at 350° (Gas mark 4) for 45 minutes.

Serve as is, or spread with butter.

Bears Biscuits

Ingredients

4 oz (113 gms) butter
4 oz (113 gms) grated coconut
4 oz (113 gms) sugar
4 oz (113 gms) ground rice
2 oz (56 gms) cornflour

Mix everything together, until it drops off the spoon. If it doesn't, add a little milk. Drop from a teaspoon into mounds on a greased baking sheet.

Bake at 350° (Gas mark 4) till light brown.

Makes about 18

When your parents have an anniversary or birthday – *you* give a dinner for *them*. (That includes leaving the kitchen spotless afterwards.)

Something-To-Sing-About Soufflé

Ingredients

4 egg yolks
5 egg whites
2 tablespoons butter or margarine
3 tablespoons flour
Dash of salt and pepper
10 tablespoons milk
½ lb (.25 kg) grated cheddar cheese

 Melt butter in pan, stir in flour till well blended. Add milk. Bring to near boiling point (but don't let it actually boil), add cheese, salt, pepper. Stir till there are no lumps and the mixture has thickened. Remove mixture from heat. Beat egg yolks. Then add them a little at a time, stirring all the while, till well mixed.

Beat egg whites till stiff.
Fold lightly into mixture.
Pour into soufflé dish (or any deep heat-proof dish).

Bake at 350° (Gas mark 4) for about 30 minutes.

 It is done when well risen and lightly brown on top. (Make sure when you look in the oven to see if it's done, that you open the door gently.)

Serve immediately.

Serves 4 generously.

Choose another F.F.F. recipe to complete your menu.

ACTORS GET-TOGETHER

Invite all the friends who are interested in acting – rehearse a play, or take it in turns to read poetry aloud. Make it a regular occasion at each other's house.

Starving Actors Soup

Ingredients

8 oz (226 gms) any kind of lentils, soaked overnight (or experiment with kidney beans, haricot beans etc.)
1 tablespoon butter
2 onions (finely chopped)
2 carrots (finely chopped)
1 pint (6 dl) chicken stock
1 potato (peeled and chopped)

Toppings: Grated raw carrot or grated raw beetroot; Spoonful of cream or yoghurt; Chopped chives.

Melt butter. Add onions and carrots. Stir for about three minutes over low heat. Add chicken stock, potato, and the drained lentils. Cook everything over low heat until ingredients are soft and mushy. Put in blender, or mash together with a large fork. Return to pan and keep warm till ready to serve. Pour into bowls and add your favourite topping. Eat with chunks of your home-made bread, heated in the oven.

Serves 4–6.

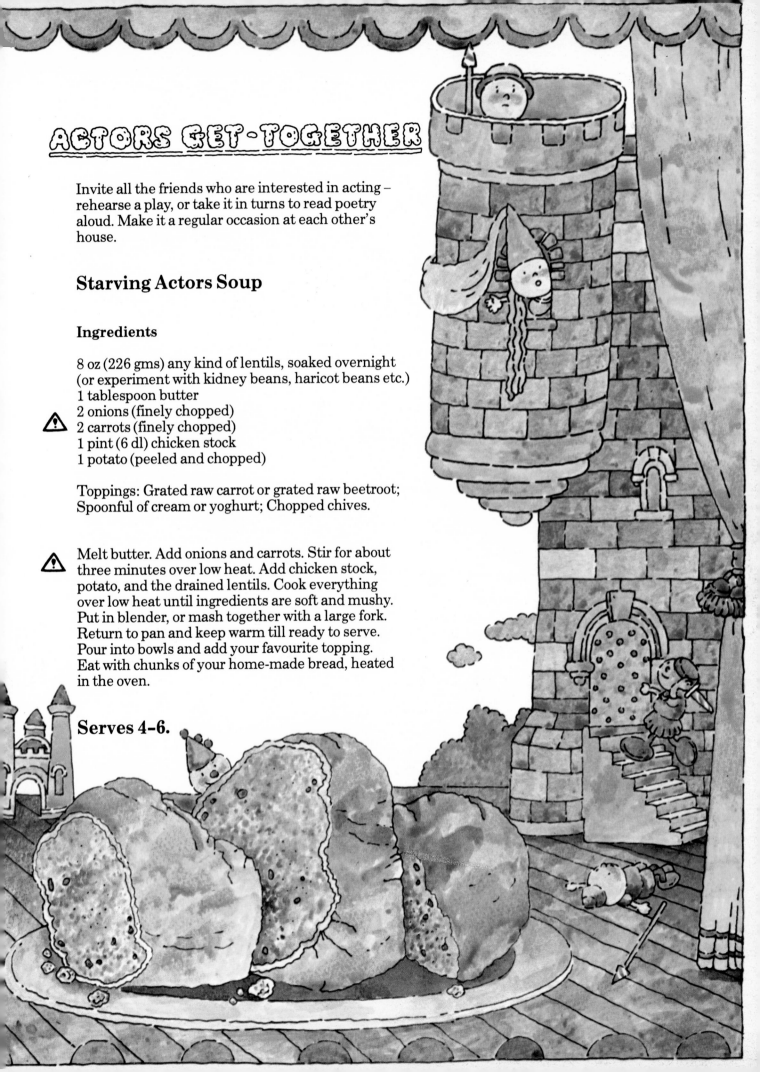

FUN FOOD FACTORY INVENTORS FEAST

Ask friends to come and create some new cookery ideas. Write them down in your own personal cookbook. Make notes of everyone's comments and do lots of experimenting.

Crazy Sandwiches

Lay out slices of wholewheat bread (one per person).
Try combinations such as:
Cream cheese, dates and sliced apple;
Grated carrot, sliced orange and sultanas;
Honey topped with sliced banana, sprinkled with sesame seeds;
Lettuce, sliced pear and grated cheese.
Invent others.

Milkshake Marvels

Mix in blender:
1 banana, ½ pint (3 dl) milk, 1 dessertspoon honey.
Blend till frothy.
Experiment with other fruits.

Instant Jam

Sliced strawberries between two thin slices of wholewheat bread and butter.

Hey Presto Peanut Butter

Ingredients

12 oz (340 gms) shelled peanuts
2 tablespoons sunflower oil
Dash of salt

Grind in blender till it's as smooth as you like it.

Banana Bonanza

Peel 1 banana per person.
Cut in half.
Stick small stick in each half.
Spread with honey, roll in any chopped nuts.
Put in freezer compartment.
Eat like ice cream.

GARDENERS DIG

Gardening is fun, particularly when you do it with friends. Plant some vegetables or herbs – in the garden or in window-boxes or pots indoors. Offer to mow the lawn, or do some digging and weeding. Work up an appetite!

Potato Peelings

Next time you are going to have mashed potatoes, offer to do the peeling. First scrub the potatoes thoroughly. Then peel carefully in thin strips, putting the peelings in cold water. When you are ready for them, pat them dry.

Heat oven to 375° (Gas mark 5). Take a baking tin and just cover the bottom with oil; heat in oven for 10 minutes. Then take out and carefully stir in peelings. Sprinkle with sea salt and bake till brown and crisp.

Drain on kitchen paper and eat immediately.

Vegetable Crunch-Up

Ingredients

1 cup grated carrot
1 cup grated white cabbage
1 cup grated red cabbage
½ cup celery, cut in thin strips
2 tablespoons oil
1 dessertspoon sugar
1 dessertspoon vinegar
Salt/pepper

Heat oil in a saucepan. When hot add carrot, cabbage and celery. Stir quickly over reasonably big heat (for 2 minutes). Add sugar. Stir again for 2 minutes. Add vinegar. Stir again. Add salt and pepper and serve. They will be hot but still deliciously crisp.

Serves 4.

PATCHWORK PARTY

Everyone brings along odd pieces of material (the more colourful the better) and you sew them together to make something – a patchwork quilt, some cushion covers, a tablecloth, and so on. Get the boys to do some cutting-out!

Patchwork Toast

Ingredients

3 slices bread (allow 1 slice at least per person)
1 egg
½ cup milk
2 tablespoons butter

Beat egg, beat in milk.
Melt butter in pan till hot (not brown).
Cut bread into 4 neat squares.
Dip in egg mixture (let excess drip off).
Put in pan and brown on both sides.
Put on heat resistant plate in warm oven.
Keep adding squares to your patchwork toast.
When finished sprinkle with brown sugar or dribble honey over the top.

(Warning – people can eat lots of these!)

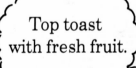

Top toast with fresh fruit.

GREATEST·CHOCOLATE·CAKE PARTY

For birthdays and other very special occasions.
Don't always leave making the birthday cake to
your mother. Make it yourself, it's great fun.

Greatest Chocolate Cake

Ingredients

4-6 oz (113-170 gms) of a carob bar (you buy it at
health stores) or plain chocolate
4 oz (113 gms) butter (softened)
4 oz (113 gms) sugar
1½ oz (42 gms) cornflour
4 eggs (separated)
2 oz (56 gms) ground almonds

**(Double quantities for a large cake but use
only 7 eggs not 8.)**

Put chocolate or carob in a small saucepan, stand
it in a larger saucepan containing hot water, put on
low heat.
Leave to melt while you:
Put butter in large bowl and beat till smooth (use
electric mixer if you have one). Add sugar. Beat till
well blended. Add flour. Beat again and add egg
yolks, one at a time. Beat well. Add ground almonds
and beat again. Add thoroughly melted chocolate
or carob. Mix together till well blended.
In another bowl, beat egg whites till they stand up
like mountains of snow. Fold lightly into chocolate
mixture till no white shows.
 Put into greased cake tin, *about* 8 inches (20 cm)
in size. Bake 45-50 minutes at 350° (Gas mark 4).

This cake is so good it really doesn't need anything
else done to it. But you can decorate it with
Chocolate Leaves.

Chocolate Leaves

4 oz (113 gms) carob or chocolate
A few rose leaves

Melt chocolate or carob the same way as before.
Spread evenly onto the underside of rose leaves.
Leave to get cold and set. Then peel off the
leaf-shaped chocolate and arrange on cake.

Be original –
decorate with
real flowers.

Collect old jars and boxes (but make sure they are clean), material, paper, glue and ribbons. Then make Honey Lemon Curd, biscuits or anything else you fancy, and package them attractively. Design your own labels, decorate the boxes, cut up material for lid covers, etc. Then give your produce to a charity or bazaar, or as Christmas presents.

Honey Lemon Curd
(enough for one small jar)

Ingredients

3 egg yolks (beaten)
3 heaped tablespoons clear honey
3 oz (85 gms) butter
2 large lemons

Melt butter in double saucepan (that is, one saucepan inside another that is filled with water). Add grated lemon rind, lemon juice and honey. Stir till melted together.
Pour slowly onto egg yolks, stirring all the time.
Return to pan, stir over gentle heat in double saucepan till it thickens (it takes ages so don't despair).
When it is as thick as double cream, cool.
Put into jar and label.

Home-made bread makes a great gift.

MIDNIGHT FEAST

Get your friends to come round with a sleeping bag or extra pillow and blanket. Then have a Midnight Feast that *doesn't* make everyone feel sick in the morning, because that's no fun at all.
Make breakfast part of the festivities.

Midnight Mouthfuls

Ingredients

8 oz (226 gms) flour
6 oz (170 gms) sugar
½ teaspoon salt
1 heaped teaspoon baking powder
1 teaspoon cinnamon
½ teaspoon nutmeg
8 tablespoons oil
 3 oz (85 gms) any mixed nuts (shelled and chopped)
2 eggs (beaten)
6 oz (170 gms) grated carrot
2–4 tablespoons apple or orange juice

Sift flour – add salt and baking powder, sugar and spices.
Add one egg and 4 tablespoons oil.
Mix.
Add the other egg and 4 tablespoons oil.
Mix again.
Add 2 tablespoons fruit juice.
Mix.
Add nuts, then carrots. Mix well.
It should then be the consistency that will drop off a spoon. If it seems too dry, add extra juice.
Grease patty tins, drop heaped dessertspoons of mixture into each one.

Bake at 350° (Gas mark 4) for 25–30 minutes.

Makes about 18.

Midnight Dip

Ingredients

3 oz (85 gms) cream cheese
2 tablespoons single cream
Sprinkling of sesame seeds
1 tablespoon chopped chives
Dash of salt and pepper
1 teaspoon paprika.

Combine cheese and cream. Add everything else and mix. Then put into a dish surrounded with strips of raw carrot, celery and cucumber, cauliflower, green and red peppers. And dip in.

BREAKFAST BEANO

A fun way to start off Saturday or Sunday (or a weekday during the holidays). Or as a follow-up to a Midnight Feast. (It could include breakfast in bed for your parents!)

Top-Of-The Morning Muesli

Before going to bed put 2 tablespoons of milk and one heaped tablespoon of oatmeal into a bowl. Stir and cover. In the morning add 1 grated apple, 1 dessertspoon of honey, 3 tablespoons of any yoghurt. Then eat.

Other things you can add if you want to: Grated rind and juice of ½ orange. Sultanas. Chopped nuts or bran. Any fruit.

Egg in Toast

Melt 1 tablespoon of butter in frying pan. Take one large slice of wholemeal bread and cut out the middle with a round biscuit cutter. Fry bread on one side. Turn over, drop egg in middle, cook till egg is done the way you like it. Add more butter if needed.

Rice 'n' Hot

Ingredients

2 breakfast cups of left-over rice
1 apple, chopped
2 cups milk
2 tablespoons honey
½ cup dried apricots, dates (chopped) or sultanas
½ teaspoon cinnamon

Put everything in pan.
Stir till hot. Then serve.

Serves 2-4.

ARTISTS GATHERING

Ask friends to bring their paints round and paint some pictures. Hold an exhibition of everyone's work. Or get ahead with next year's Christmas cards.

Arty Crafty Chicken Salad

Ingredients

Take some left-over cooked chicken (enough to fill a large cup), remove skin and cut in strips. Sprinkle lightly with salt and pepper.

Add at least *one* of the following:

 1 tablespoon green
or red peppers
½ chicory
2 sticks celery
} all sliced into thin strips

Then add <u>one</u> of these fruits, whichever you happen to have:

1 peach
1 apple
1 pear
} sliced thinly

Mix carefully with some Arty Crafty dressing. Decorate with mint leaves, or chopped nuts, or sunflower or sesame seeds. Or top with cottage cheese. And serve on a bed of lettuce or watercress.

Arty Crafty Dressing

Ingredients

1 small carton plain yoghurt
1 teaspoon lemon juice
1 teaspoon honey
1 teaspoon finely chopped spring onion (optional)
1 teaspoon of your favourite herb
Salt and pepper

Mix well with a fork and pour some over your salad – judge for yourself how much you like.

Serves 2

Invite your grandparents or some old people who don't get out much to come for tea. Give them a lovely time. If the old people live within walking distance, go with your friends to collect them. Then take them home.

Granny's Loaf

Ingredients

6 oz (170 gms) butter
6 oz (170 gms) sugar
3 eggs (beaten)
8 oz (226 gms) flour (sifted)
2 teaspoons baking powder
Grated rind or orange*
1 banana (sliced thinly)
2 oz (56 gms) ground almonds*
2 oz (56 gms) chopped mixed nuts*
2 oz (56 gms) dessicated coconut*

Cream together butter and sugar really well.
Add beaten eggs, cream together thoroughly.
Add baking powder to flour.
Then add flour, almonds, nuts, bananas,
orange rind, coconut – in any order you like.
Mix everything till well blended.
Grease a loaf tin. Spoon mixture into it.

Bake at 325° (Gas mark 3) for about 1 hour,
15 minutes.

Serve sliced, plain or buttered.

Any two of the ingredients marked with an asterisk can be left out. Or you can alter the quantities to suit your taste. Try lemon peel instead of orange peel, or dates rather than nuts. Whatever you fancy. Experiment. See what you can think of.

Helping others is fun.

CHRISTMAS TREE DECORATING PARTY

It's easy to make a party out of decorating the Christmas tree, especially if you share it with your friends. Make some biscuits to eat while decorating, or to use as decorations themselves.

Tree Biscuits (hand-made)

Ingredients

1 egg
8 oz (226 gms) butter or margarine (softened)
4 oz (113 gms) sugar
1½ teaspoons cinnamon (powdered)
1½ teaspoons nutmeg (powdered)
1 teaspoon cloves (powdered)
½ teaspoon salt
1 teaspoon vanilla essence
1 dessertspoon milk
12 oz (340 gms) sifted flour

(You can add a small handful of chopped nuts, sultanas or currants, or lemon or orange peel, if you want.)

Put everything except flour into a large bowl. Then add flour and mix with clean hands. Wrap dough in greaseproof paper and put into fridge till it is cold (or as long as you can bear to wait).

Take smallish pieces of dough and pat on to a well-floured board, gently, till about ¼ inch (0.6 cm) thick. Then cut out or make your favourite shapes (make a hole at the top if you are going to tie a ribbon through the biscuit to hang on the tree). Put on lightly-greased baking tray and bake for about 12 minutes at 350° (Gas mark 4), till slightly browned. Remove, leave to cool a little, then take off tray to cool completely. Tie on ribbon and hang on tree if you are going to eat biscuits same day. If not, wrap biscuits in see-through film, leaving enough film at the top to tie the ribbon around. Then tie on to tree with a bow. You will see the shape of the biscuit through the film, and they will keep fresh like that for several days while making the tree look pretty. Choose brightly coloured ribbon.

String some popcorn on the tree.

It depends on how large you make the biscuits as to how many you get.

AND THIS IS WHERE YOU'LL FIND US

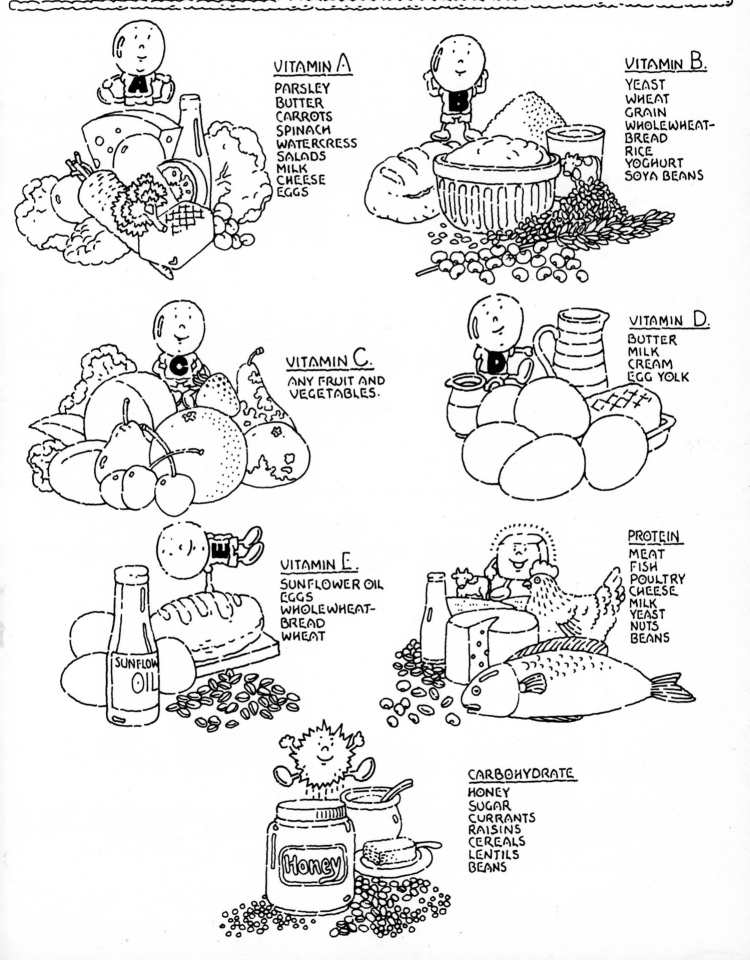

VITAMIN A

PARSLEY
BUTTER
CARROTS
SPINACH
WATERCRESS
SALADS
MILK
CHEESE
EGGS

VITAMIN B.

YEAST
WHEAT
GRAIN
WHOLEWHEAT-
BREAD
RICE
YOGHURT
SOYA BEANS

VITAMIN C.

ANY FRUIT AND
VEGETABLES.

VITAMIN D.

BUTTER
MILK
CREAM
EGG YOLK

VITAMIN E.

SUNFLOWER OIL
EGGS
WHOLEWHEAT-
BREAD
WHEAT

PROTEIN

MEAT
FISH
POULTRY
CHEESE
MILK
YEAST
NUTS
BEANS

CARBOHYDRATE

HONEY
SUGAR
CURRANTS
RAISINS
CEREALS
LENTILS
BEANS